The Multiplier's Mindset

Thinking Differently ABOUT DISCIPLESHIP

with

Cynthia Anderson

VIDEO COURSE COMPANION WORKBOOK

C O N T E N T S

THE MULTIPLIER'S MINDSET

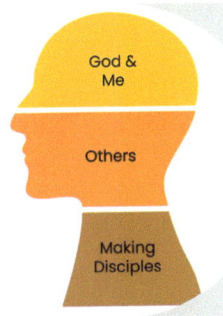

INTRODUCTION

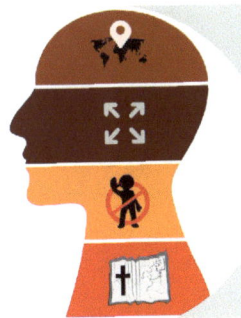

ALIGN WITH TRUTH

What We Believe About God and Ourselves

ADJUST YOUR PERSPECTIVE

What We Believe About Others

ADAPT STRATEGIES

What We Believe About How to Make Disciples

CYNTHIA ANDERSON

INTRODUCTION

Welcome to the incredible joy of multiplying disciples of our Lord Jesus! When you have the privilege of leading even *one* person into a relationship with Christ, that is amazing. Our God, in His nature, is a God of multiplication. He wants to *multiply* that joy and use you to see His Kingdom grow **exponentially**.

In this course, as you adjust your mindsets and actively pursue multiplication rather than addition, God will empower you to do what previously was thought impossible.

Enjoy the journey ahead!

- CYNTHIA

INSTRUCTIONS FOR

GROUP LEADERS

DEAR LEADER-

Thank you for stepping up to lead this study! Your role as a facilitator is invaluable in guiding our discussions on *The Multiplier's Mindset: Thinking Differently About Discipleship*. Each week, except for the first where we'll start with a video, we'll delve into the chapters we've read together.

Your presence is key. You'll be modeling participatory learning, a cornerstone of disciple multiplication. Don't worry about being an expert; often, your silence creates space for others to share. Encourage everyone to participate, even if they haven't fully completed their homework. Remember, there are no wrong answers—let's make this a safe space for exploration and growth.

Each week, participants will read chapters, journal in this workbook, and tackle at least two action steps. Your example is crucial here. By sharing your successes and failures, you'll create an environment where others feel safe to experiment too.

Here's a simple weekly plan:

1. Check-In (5 minutes): Start with personal updates and prayer needs.
2. Content Review (15 minutes): Discuss highlights from the chapters. Feel free to go chapter by chapter or address overarching themes.
3. Action Review (10 minutes): Reflect on action steps taken. Celebrate successes and offer support where needed.
4. Video (approximately 10 minutes): Watch the provided video together.
5. Prayer and Send-Off (5 minutes): Close with a prayer for God's power upon the group as you put this week's training into action.

Your leadership will inspire meaningful engagement and discipleship. Thank you for being part of this journey!

Join other readers online:

Cynthia Anderson

GROW THE KINGDOM!

LESSON ONE

Watch Video 1- Introduction & Faith, Expand, and Enough Mindsets

DISCUSSION:
Group Leaders - Start with an Ice-breaker. *What is your favorite animal or the most unusual animal you've ever seen before?*

ASK YOURSELF

WRITE YOUR ANSWERS HERE...

What brought you to this study? Share what sparked your interest or what you hope to learn.

Tell us about your faith journey and experiences with discipleship. If you're currently mentoring others, let us know!

Discuss the difference between multiplication and addition mindsets. Share your initial thoughts on this concept. *(If time allows)*

THIS WEEK'S ASSIGNMENTS:

1 **TO READ:**
Read the Introduction and Chapters 1-5 (pages 1-60).

2 **TO JOURNAL:**
Journal about the questions at the end of the chapters.

3 **FOR GROUPS:**
Choose at least 2 suggested action steps in the workbook (grey box at the bottom of each chapter's page) to report back to the group about.

CHAPTER ONE: STRUGGLE

Scripture: *Hope deferred makes the heart sick, but desire fulfilled is a tree of life.*
—Proverbs 13:12, NASB

Key Concepts:
- God loves to work through ordinary people whom others would often discredit.
- Without a disciple and church multiplication approach, population growth among the unreached will outdistance church growth.
- Changing your thinking changes your actions, which changes your results.

JOURNAL ABOUT THESE QUESTIONS:

CAN YOU IDENTIFY WITH THE AUTHOR'S STRUGGLE TO BELIEVE FOR SOMETHING FAR BEYOND HER OWN ABILITY? IN WHAT WAY?

WHAT MADE THE DIFFERENCE FOR ANDERSON AND GAVE HER COURAGE TO BELIEVE GOD FOR GREATER THINGS?

THINK ABOUT ANY OLD HABITS OR WAYS OF THINKING YOU'RE ALREADY QUESTIONING OR EXPLORING. HOW HAVE YOU NOTICED GOD BEGINNING TO SHIFT YOUR BELIEFS OR MINDSET?

SUGGESTED ACTION STEPS:

Reflect on a past dream. Spend 10-15 minutes journaling about a dream you once had but let go of. Write down your thoughts, feelings, and anything God might be speaking to you about it.

Research local demographics. Take a moment to search online for any unreached people or immigrant communities in your area. Note their current population and growth rate, and compare it to the growth rate of churches in your area or country.

CHAPTER TWO: CHANGE

Scripture: *Do not conform any longer to the pattern of this world, but be transformed by the renewing of your mind.* –Romans 12:2

Key Concepts:
- Provocative questions asked by key mentors spark change in our lives.
- Crisis, hopelessness, and "dark nights of the soul" make us willing and ready to be transformed.
- Peter went through multiple mindset shifts as Jesus formed and shaped him.
- Encounters with God in Scripture also play a key role in bringing about change in us.

JOURNAL ABOUT THESE QUESTIONS:

WHAT SHIFTS OF THINKING TOOK PLACE IN PETER'S LIFE? HOW DID THOSE COME ABOUT? WHAT IMPACT DID THEY HAVE?

EXPLORE HOW DR. VICTOR CHOUDHRIE'S VIEWS ON CHURCH PLANTING CHANGED OVER TIME. WHAT LESSONS CAN WE GLEAN FROM HIS JOURNEY?

WHAT HOPE OR EXPECTATION CAUSED YOU TO READ THIS BOOK?
Take time to submit those hopes or expectations to the Lord, and ask Him to use what you are about to read to bring about the changes He desires in order to release His full purposes through you.

SUGGESTED ACTION STEPS:

Reflect on readiness for change. Spend time in prayer, asking God to prepare you for transformation as you delve into this book.

Discuss with someone close to you. Talk with a friend, spouse, or colleague about your current thoughts and methods in discipleship. Share areas where you're open to change and eager to discover more effective approaches to disciple-making.

HOW WE THINK ABOUT GOD and OURSELVES

Multiplier's Mindset- Part 1

Mindsets About God & Ourselves- *Align with Truth*

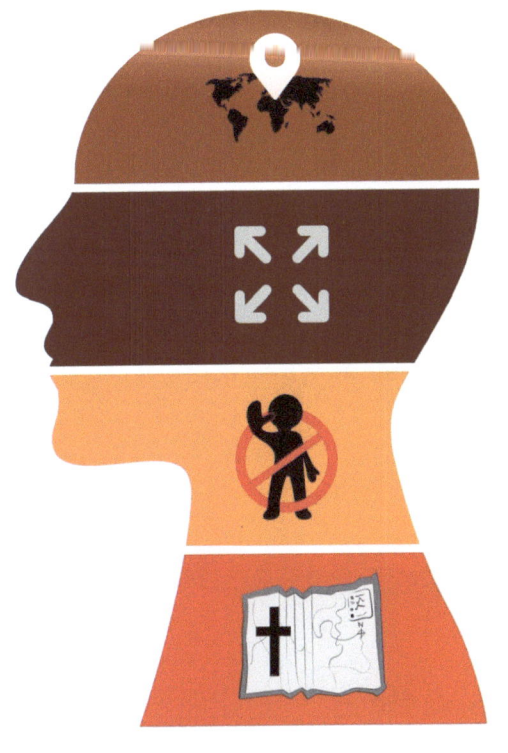

F — Faith

God can do it here. God can do it through me.

E — Expand

Don't ask for schoolbooks when God can give you a Tata truck.

E — Enough

I don't need more stuff. I already have enough.

D — Discover

Don't bring the Gospel to save the lost, discover the Gospel at work in the lost.

ALIGN WITH TRUTH

CHAPTER THREE: FAITH

Scripture: *You will receive power after the Holy Spirit comes upon you; and you will be my witnesses in Jerusalem, and in Judea, and Samaria, and to the ends of the earth.* –Acts 1:8

Key Concepts:
- God can do it here. God can do it through me.
- Intellectual assent to God's desire to reach the nations is not enough.
- Many do not fulfill the Great Commission because they do not know about it or that it involves them.
- Scripture affirms God's ability to do extraordinary things through ordinary people.

JOURNAL ABOUT THESE QUESTIONS:

IN WHAT WAYS HAVE YOU STRUGGLED TO BELIEVE GOD COULD USE YOU TO SEE DISCIPLES MULTIPLY RAPIDLY? HOW DOES THIS CHAPTER SPEAK TO THOSE STRUGGLES?

ON A SCALE OF 1 TO 5, RATE YOUR LEVEL OF FAITH IN BELIEVING GOD COULD MULTIPLY MANY NEW DISCIPLES OR START A MOVEMENT THROUGH YOU AND THOSE YOU TRAIN?

THE CHAPTER PRESENTS IDEAS FOR GROWING FAITH IN MULTIPLYING DISCIPLES. WHICH RESONATES WITH YOU? WHEN WILL YOU START?

SUGGESTED ACTION STEPS:

Reflect on obstacles. *Discuss with a trusted friend or journal about reasons or excuses that may have hindered your impact as a disciple.*

Memorize Scripture. *Commit to memorizing a Scripture verse from this chapter or any other verse that strengthens your faith in God for greater things.*

CHAPTER FOUR: EXPAND

Scripture: *The LORD answered me, and said, Write the vision, and make it plain upon tables, that he may run that readeth it.* –Habbakuk 2:2, KJV.

Key Concepts:

• Those who see movements embrace a God-sized vision. Their mindset shifts from what they can do to what God can do through them and the many others whom they mobilize.

• Writing down an End Vision statement about the future will help one take action now that leads to multiplication later.

• God wants to bring about transformation, not only multiply Christians or churches.

JOURNAL ABOUT THESE QUESTIONS:

Dream size reflection.
Consider the size of your current dream. Is it God-sized or something achievable by you and your church? How might God want to expand it even further?

Vision alignment.
When setting goals and envisioning the future, are you focusing on the needs of the lost or primarily on your desires? How could you adjust your mindset to prioritize reaching the lost?

Farmer and sons reflection.
Think about the story of the farmer and his three sons. Which son do you relate to the most and why?

SUGGESTED ACTION STEPS:

Prayerful exploration. *Take a prayer drive through your area and ask God what He desires to accomplish there. Write down your insights in a journal. Consider sketching a simple diagram envisioning disciple-multiplication across multiple churches.*

Calculate multiplication potential. *Use a calculator to explore the potential impact of starting five groups that multiply. Estimate the number of groups by the fourth and tenth generations.*

CHAPTER FIVE: ENOUGH

Scripture: *His divine power has given us everything we need for life and godliness through our knowledge of Him who called us by His own glory and goodness.* –2 Peter 1:3

Key Concepts:
- I don't need more stuff. I already have enough.
- God knows what we need—more than, and before, we know what we need.
- More people, money, expertise, equipment, etc. do not automatically equal greater fruitfulness.
- If we want to see greater results, we may need to do things differently.

JOURNAL ABOUT THESE QUESTIONS:

HOW MIGHT YOUR CHILDHOOD EXPERIENCES BE INFLUENCING YOUR UNDERSTANDING OF GOD AS AN ABLE AND GENEROUS PROVIDER?

WHERE DO YOU STRUGGLE TO BELIEVE THAT YOU HAVE ENOUGH TO ACCOMPLISH WHAT GOD IS CALLING YOU TO DO?

WHAT MIGHT GOD BE PROMPTING YOU TO DO DIFFERENTLY WITH WHAT HE HAS ALREADY GIVEN?

SUGGESTED ACTION STEPS:

Surrendering needs to God. List the things you believe you need to fulfill God's vision. Pray over this list, trusting God's provision even without these items. Quietly listen for the Holy Spirit's reassurance of your sufficiency in Him.

Recognizing available resources. Create a second list of the resources you already possess for God's work. Consider how you can multiply or use them differently for greater impact. Listen attentively for the Holy Spirit's guidance in this process.

ACTION STEPS

Which Action Steps did you work on this week? *Be ready to share with your group about at least two of them and how they went for you.*

ACTION STEP CHECKLIST

- ☐ Reflect on a past dream.

- ☐ Research local demographics.

- ☐ Reflect on readiness for change.

- ☐ Discuss with someone close to you.

- ☐ Reflect on obstacles.

- ☐ Memorize scripture.

- ☐ Prayerful exploration.

- ☐ Calculate multiplication potential.

- ☐ Surrendering needs to God.

- ☐ Recognizing available resources.

NOTES

Congratulations! You have made significant steps forward this past week. As you meet with your group and discuss together, God will solidify these lessons in your heart and mind. Keep up the great work. As we do our part, surrendering our minds and hearts to Him, He brings the transformation we so desire.

LESSON TWO

Watch Video 2- Start Making Disciples – Discover, Grow, Leaders, & Open Mindsets

DISCUSSION.

ASK YOURSELF

WRITE YOUR ANSWERS HERE...

Prayer Requests. What are some personal prayer needs you have this week? If in a group setting, how can you pray for your group this week?

Content Review.
What stood out to you in the chapters we read this week?

Action Item Review. Share about any application or action steps taken after reading. Discuss how these steps went, what went well, and what challenges were faced.

THIS WEEK'S ASSIGNMENTS:

1 **TO READ:**
Read Chapters 6-9 (pages 61-94).

2 **TO JOURNAL:**
Journal about the questions at the end of the chapters.

3 **FOR GROUPS:**
Choose at least 2 suggested action steps in the workbook to report back to the group about.

CHAPTER SIX: DISCOVER

Scripture: *My Father is always working, and now I am working too.* –John 5:17

Key Concepts:
Don't bring the gospel to save the lost. Discover the gospel at work in the lost.
• God is already at work in your area and people group. He is actively revealing Himself and drawing people towards a knowledge of His love.
• A Savior mentality (we are there to bring salvation to others) gets in the way of discovering what God is already doing in hearts and lives.

JOURNAL ABOUT THESE QUESTIONS:

HAVE YOU EVER FOCUSED ON "BRINGING THE GOSPEL" TO OTHERS, RATHER THAN LOOKING WHERE GOD IS ALREADY AT WORK? HOW MIGHT SHIFTING THIS MINDSET IMPACT YOUR APPROACH?

THINK OF A TIME WHEN YOU'VE SEEN GOD AT WORK AROUND YOU IN SOMEONE'S LIFE. HOW DID YOU PARTNER WITH GOD AS YOU NOTICED THIS?

DO YOU NOTICE ANY SIGNS OF GOD AT WORK IN YOUR NEIGHBORHOOD OR COMMUNITY? HOW COULD YOU FOCUS ATTENTION AND ENERGY THERE RATHER THAN STARTING SOMETHING IN YOUR OWN STRENGTH?

SUGGESTED ACTION STEPS:

Seek God's Work in Current Events: *Scan a newspaper or news website to discern where God might be at work in the world. Consider what new ministry opportunities He may be orchestrating that you haven't noticed before.*

Observe God's Kindness Daily: *Pay close attention to people and situations throughout your day. Look for signs of God's kindness or love behind the scenes. Ask Him to reveal how you can partner with His ongoing work around you.*

PART 2

HOW WE THINK ABOUT OTHERS

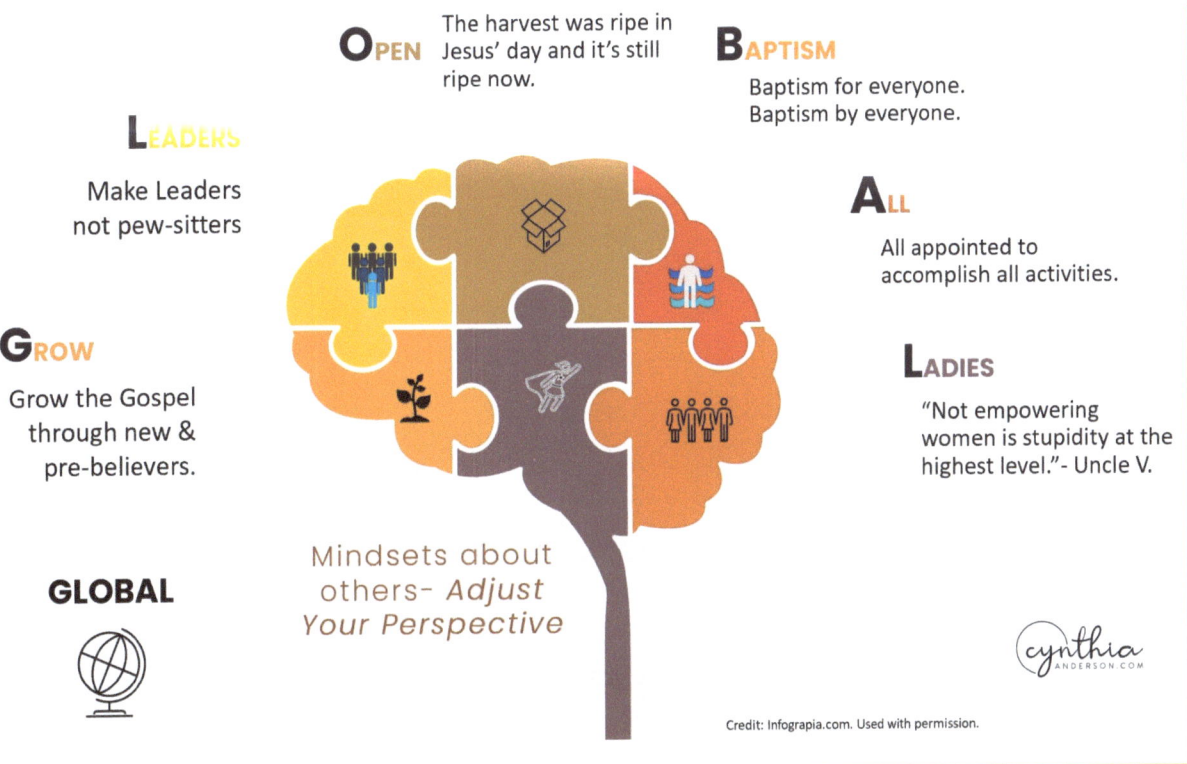

OPEN — The harvest was ripe in Jesus' day and it's still ripe now.

BAPTISM — Baptism for everyone. Baptism by everyone.

LEADERS — Make Leaders not pew-sitters

ALL — All appointed to accomplish all activities.

GROW — Grow the Gospel through new & pre-believers.

LADIES — "Not empowering women is stupidity at the highest level."- Uncle V.

GLOBAL

Mindsets about others- *Adjust Your Perspective*

cynthia
ANDERSON.COM

Credit: Infograpia.com. Used with permission.

ADJUST YOUR PERSPECTIVE

CHAPTER SEVEN: GROW

Scripture: *Come, see a man who told me everything I ever did. Could this be the Messiah?*
–John 4:29

Key Concepts:
- Followers must become fishermen.
- Church members come and sit. Disciples go and do.
- Fruit can become fruitful.
- Change religion, change a person. Change allegiance, change a community.

JOURNAL ABOUT THESE QUESTIONS:

WHAT IS THE DIFFERENCE BETWEEN A CONVERT AND A DISCIPLE? WHY IS A MINDSET SHIFT IN THIS AREA SO IMPORTANT IF WE WANT TO SEE MULTIPLICATION?

IN YOUR CONTEXT, DO YOU NORMALLY SEE PEOPLE MAKING CONVERTS OR DISCIPLES? WHAT EXAMPLES CAN YOU GIVE OF EACH?

HOW MIGHT IMMEDIATE BAPTISM IMPACT YOUR APPROACH TO CALLING PEOPLE TO FOLLOW CHRIST? DOES IT SEEM FEASIBLE OR NOT, AND WHY?

SUGGESTED ACTION STEPS:

Differentiate Between Discipleship and Conversion: *Talk with a friend about the distinction between making disciples and making converts. Assess which of these you're presently focused on and pray together about any necessary adjustments.*

Pray for Transformation: *Lift up in prayer those in your church or group who appear to be converts rather than disciples. Ask God to empower you to influence a shift in the community, leading to more individuals becoming active participants in spreading the faith, not just followers.*

CHAPTER EIGHT: LEADERS

Scripture: *"Come, follow me,"* Jesus said, *"and I will send you out to fish for people."*
– Matthew 4:19

Key Concepts:
- Train leaders, not seat-fillers.
- There is a great difference between a convert and a disciple. Make disciples.
- The word conversion has negative implications having to do with leaving your family and community.
- There are three important callings for the person choosing to follow Christ.

JOURNAL ABOUT THESE QUESTIONS:

WHAT IS THE DIFFERENCE BETWEEN A CONVERT AND A DISCIPLE? WHY IS A MINDSET SHIFT IN THIS AREA SO IMPORTANT IF WE WANT TO SEE MULTIPLICATION?

IN YOUR CONTEXT, DO YOU NORMALLY SEE PEOPLE MAKING CONVERTS OR DISCIPLES? TRAINING LEADERS OR ONLY PEW-SITTERS? GIVE EXAMPLES OF EACH.

HOW MIGHT IMMEDIATE BAPTISM IMPACT YOUR APPROACH TO CALLING PEOPLE TO FOLLOW CHRIST? DOES IT SEEM FEASIBLE OR NOT, AND WHY?

SUGGESTED ACTION STEPS:

Reflect on Invitation: *Recall the last time you led someone to Christ. How did you invite them? If you have never led someone to Christ, reflect on how you would invite them to follow Jesus.*

Explore Callings: *Think about the three callings for sharing the good news. Journal your thoughts and practice giving a gospel invitation with them in mind.*

Discuss Baptism: *Talk with those you're mentoring about baptism's meaning. Baptize those ready to take this step of faith.*

CHAPTER NINE: OPEN

Scripture: *Don't you have a saying, "It's still four months until harvest"? I tell you, open your eyes and look at the fields! They are ripe for harvest.* –John 4:35

Key Concepts:
- The harvest was ripe in Jesus' time, and it's still ripe now.
- Untested assumptions about someone's openness prevent us from attempting to share the gospel.
- If God is the same, yesterday, today, and forever, then God is the same here where we live too.

JOURNAL ABOUT THESE QUESTIONS:

WHAT ASSUMPTIONS DO YOU MAKE ABOUT LOST PEOPLE AROUND YOU? ARE THERE ANY ETHNIC GROUPS OR CLASSES OF PEOPLE YOU TEND TO ASSUME ARE NOT RIPE FOR THE GOSPEL? IF SO, HAVE YOU TESTED THOSE ASSUMPTIONS BY SHARING WITH THEM?

CONSIDER PAST EXPERIENCES AND WHAT OTHERS HAVE TOLD YOU ABOUT THE LOST IN YOUR AREA. DO THESE EXPERIENCES MAKE YOU MORE HOPEFUL OR DOUBTFUL ABOUT THE READINESS OF PEOPLE TO BECOME DISCIPLES?

WHAT IS GOD SAYING TO YOU ABOUT THE HARVEST? REREAD JOHN 4 AND ASK HIM TO REVEAL HIS MESSAGE TO YOU FROM THESE VERSES.

SUGGESTED ACTION STEPS:

Challenge Assumptions: *Reflect on and repent of any untested assumptions about your neighbors' openness to the Good News.*

Prayer for the Unresponsive: *Pray daily this week for the people you've deemed closed or resistant to your message.*

Act in Faith: *Stay alert for chances to show kindness, offer prayer, or share your story with those around you. Trust that God has prepared some of them to listen and believe.*

NOTES

_____
_____
_____
_____
_____
_____
_____
_____
_____
_____
_____
_____
_____
_____
_____
_____
_____
_____
_____
_____
_____
_____

ACTION STEPS

Which Action Steps did you work on this week? Be ready to share with your group about at least two of them and how they went for you.

ACTION STEP CHECKLIST

- ☐ Seek God's work in current events.

- ☐ Observe God's kindness daily.

- ☐ Differentiate between discipleship and conversion.

- ☐ Pray for transformation.

- ☐ Reflect on invitation.

- ☐ Explore callings.

- ☐ Discuss baptism.

- ☐ Challenge assumptions.

- ☐ Prayer for the unresponsive.

- ☐ Act in faith.

NOTES

Reflect on how God is already working in your community and among those you interact with. Shift from a mindset of bringing the gospel to discovering where God is already revealing Himself. Embrace the journey of discerning His work in hearts and lives.

LESSON THREE

Watch Video 3- Who Are the Ministers? Baptism, All, & Ladies Mindset Shifts

DISCUSSION:

ASK YOURSELF

WRITE YOUR ANSWERS HERE...

Prayer Requests. What are some personal prayer needs you have this week? If In a group setting, how can you pray for your group this week?

Content Review.
What stood out to you in the chapters we read this week?

Action Item Review. Share about any application or action steps taken after reading. Discuss how these steps went, what went well, and what challenges were faced.

THIS WEEK'S ASSIGNMENTS:

1 **TO READ:**
Read chapters 10-12 (pages 95-130).

2 **TO JOURNAL:**
Journal about the questions at the end of the chapters.

3 **FOR GROUPS:**
Choose at least 2 suggested action steps in the workbook to report back to the group about.

CHAPTER TEN: BAPTISM

Scripture: *As they traveled along the road, they came to some water and the eunuch said, "Look, here is water. What can stand in the way of my being baptized?"* –Acts 8:36

Key Concepts:
• Baptism for all, baptism by all.
• In the New Testament, we find many examples of ordinary people baptizing others.
• Clergy control through restrictions related to church ordinances, like baptism, hinders rather than advances the multiplication of disciples in a region.

JOURNAL ABOUT THESE QUESTIONS:

WHICH OF THE THREE SCRIPTURE VERSES GIVEN DID YOU FIND MOST HELPFUL IN UNDERSTANDING THIS ISSUE? ARE THERE ANY OTHER PASSAGES THAT COME TO MIND AS YOU CONSIDER THIS?

CONSIDER THE EXAMPLE GIVEN OF THE BELIEVERS IN THE HIGH MOUNTAINS OF NEPAL. WHAT WOULD YOU DO IN THIS KIND OF SITUATION TO HELP PEOPLE BE ABLE TO OBEY JESUS AND FOLLOW HIM IN BAPTISM?

WHAT QUESTIONS DO YOU STILL HAVE CONCERNING THIS ISSUE? WHAT WOULD HOLD YOU BACK OR PROPEL YOU FORWARD TOWARD RELEASING ORDINARY, NON-ORDAINED PEOPLE TO BAPTIZE OTHERS?

SUGGESTED ACTION STEPS:

Reflect and Discuss: *Prayerfully reflect on any concerns or fears you may have about baptism. Discuss them with your group or spouse and search Scripture verses related to the topic.*

Survey Perspectives: *Survey friends and family about their views on baptism. Ask what it means to them and who they believe should be able to baptize others, and why.*

Act in Obedience: *Baptize new believers who haven't yet taken this step of obedience to Christ's command.*

CHAPTER ELEVEN: ALL

Scripture: *You are a chosen people, a royal priesthood, a holy nation, God's special possession, that you may declare the praises of him who called you out of darkness into his wonderful light.* −1 Peter 2:9

Key Concepts:
• All are appointed to accomplish all activities.
• Failure to equip and release the laity to do the work of the ministry is a major cause of church decline that we cannot afford to ignore.
• According to Ephesians 4:11–12, the role of apostles, prophets, evangelists, pastors, and teachers is to equip the saints to do the work of the ministry.
• Embracing a new mindset about the priesthood of all believers is critical for disciple multiplication to take place.

JOURNAL ABOUT THESE QUESTIONS:

What is your understanding of the priesthood of all believers as described in 1 Peter? What steps could be taken to help local believers flow in their gifts and calling as royal priests of God?

▷

If you are a professional missionary or pastor, what percentage of your time do you give to equipping, mentoring, modeling, and raising up others? How could you increase that in the coming year?

▷

How could you make greater space for every disciple to recognize, activate and grow in using their spiritual gifts both in the church and in their community?

▷

SUGGESTED ACTION STEPS:

Affirmation Outreach: *Write a note of encouragement or make a phone call to a layperson, affirming their identity and value as a minister in the Kingdom.*

Create Space For All: *Look for creative ways to intentionally make room for ordinary believers to develop and utilize their spiritual gifts..*

CHAPTER TWELVE:LADIES

Scripture: *"When Priscilla and Aquilla heard him [Apollos], they invited him to their home and explained to him the way of God more adequately."* –Acts 18:26

Key Concepts:
• Not empowering women is stupidity at the highest level. –Victor Choudhrie
• In Scripture, and historically, we find abundant evidence of God using women to disciple and influence many.
• Women can be effective disciple multipliers. Not mobilizing and empowering them is a costly and ineffective strategy.

JOURNAL ABOUT THESE QUESTIONS:

HOW HAVE YOU OPENED DOORS FOR WOMEN IN YOUR CIRCLE OF INFLUENCE TO SERVE AS TRAINERS, COACHES, OR DISCIPLE-MAKERS? IF A WOMAN, WHO OPENED DOORS OF OPPORTUNITY FOR YOU?

WHAT STOOD OUT TO YOU FROM THE LIFE OF MABEL LOSSING JONES, OR HENRIETTA MEARS?

WHAT WILL YOU DO TO ENSURE THAT WOMEN FEEL EMPOWERED AND RELEASED TO USE THEIR GOD-GIVEN TALENTS TO MULTIPLY DISCIPLES OR TO FURTHER EQUIP WOMEN WITH DISCIPLE-MAKING AND LEADERSHIP SKILLS?

SUGGESTED ACTION STEPS:

Empower Women: Open doors for women in your life to use their gifts. Provide a platform for them to speak and make space at your table of influence to invite their voice and ideas.

Support Young Moms: Recognize the busy schedules of many women. Help young moms who are interested in ministry by offering assistance with childcare or other tasks, enabling them to engage more fully in disciple-making and active ministry roles.

LESSON THREE

NOTES

_____

_____

_____

_____

_____

_____

_____

_____

_____

_____

_____

_____

_____

_____

_____

_____

_____

_____

_____

_____

_____

ACTION STEPS

Which Action Steps did you work on this week? Be ready to share with your group about at least two of them and how they went for you.

This week, add In your own action steps you have committed to from your lessons.

ACTION STEP CHECKLIST

- ☐ Reflect and discuss concerns or fears.
- ☐ Survey perspectives.
- ☐ Act in obedience - baptize new believers.
- ☐ Affirmation outreach.
- ☐ Create space for gift development and use.
- ☐ Empower women.
- ☐ Support young moms.
- ☐
- ☐
- ☐

NOTES

Explore the concept of baptism as a communal and inclusive act within the faith community. Consider the New Testament examples where ordinary believers baptized others. Reflect on how removing unnecessary barriers can foster greater disciple multiplication in your context.

LESSON FOUR

Watch Video 4- Different Discipleship Processes: Prayer, In Groups & Ongoing

DISCUSSION:

ASK YOURSELF

WRITE YOUR ANSWERS HERE...

Prayer Requests. What are some personal prayer needs you have this week? If In a group setting, how can you pray for your group this week?

Content Review.
What stood out to you in the chapters we read this week?

Action Item Review. Share about any application or action steps taken after reading. Discuss how these steps went, what went well, and what challenges were faced.

THIS WEEK'S ASSIGNMENTS:

1 **TO READ:**
Read Chapters 13-15 (pages 131-155).

2 **TO JOURNAL:**
Journal about the questions at the end of the chapters.

3 **FOR GROUPS:**
Choose at least 2 suggested action steps in the workbook to report back to the group about.

WHAT WE BELIEVE ABOUT HOW TO MAKE DISCIPLES

Multiplier's Mindset- Part 3
Mindsets about Making Disciples - *Adapt Strategies*

PRAYER

Prayer is power not a prelude

IN GROUPS

Individuals → Addition
Groups → Multiplication

ONGOING

It's a process, not a program.

NEEDS

Ownership above offers.

EASY

Keep it easy and actionable.

EQUIPPERS

Equip equippers.
Disciple disciple-makers.

RELEVANT

Participatory, culturally relevant
worship spreads far.

PIONEER

Credit: Infograpia.com. Used with permission.

ADAPT STRATEGIES

CHAPTER THIRTEEN:PRAYER

Scripture: *Jesus told his disciples . . .that they should always pray and never give up."* –
Luke 18:1 NIV

Key Concepts:
- Prayer is ministry, not a prelude to ministry.
- Wherever there is evidence of a significant move of God, we find behind it those who faithfully devoted themselves to prayer.
- Prayer walking, using a Lost & Saved list, and many other means can be used to cultivate extraordinary prayer for the lost of your area.

JOURNAL ABOUT THESE QUESTIONS:

HOW EXTRAORDINARY WOULD YOU SAY YOUR PRAYER LIFE IS TODAY? WHAT WOULD YOU LIKE TO SEE IT BECOME IN THE NEXT FEW MONTHS OR YEAR?

WHAT DO YOU MOST ENJOY ABOUT PRAYER? WHAT DO YOU FIND MOST DIFFICULT IN LIVING A LIFE OF FAITHFUL PRAYER?

HAVE YOU EVER USED A PRAYER SYSTEM OR STRUCTURE TO HELP YOU DEVELOP A REGULAR PRAYER HABIT? HOW DID IT HELP OR HINDER YOUR PRAYER LIFE?

SUGGESTED ACTION STEPS:

Establish a New Prayer Habit: *Think about starting a new personal or group prayer routine in the coming months.*

Use a Prayer App: *Install a prayer app on your phone, like the one from <u>Joshua Project</u>, to remind you to pray for unreached people or for contemplative prayer.*

Attend a Different Prayer Meeting: *Visit a prayer gathering that you don't usually attend to broaden your prayer experience.*

CHAPTER FOURTEEN: IN GROUPS

Scripture: *As for me and my household, we will serve the Lord.* – Joshua 24:15

Key Concepts:
- Individuals   Addition, Groups   Multiplication
- American individualism is not necessarily biblical or in line with Scripture.
- Extraction versus entry evangelism.
- *Oikos* and households coming to faith together is the primary biblical model.

JOURNAL ABOUT THESE QUESTIONS:

HOW DOES YOUR CULTURAL WORLDVIEW OR OWN DISCIPLESHIP EXPERIENCE INFLUENCE YOU IN RELATIONSHIP TO MAKING DISCIPLES INDIVIDUALLY OR IN GROUPS?

WHICH OF THE BENEFITS OF DISCIPLING IN GROUPS STANDS OUT TO YOU AS BEING MOST IMPORTANT? WHY?

WHAT IS "EXTRACTION EVANGELISM", AND HOW IS IT A BARRIER TO THE MULTIPLICATION OF DISCIPLES?

SUGGESTED ACTION STEPS:

Reflect on Your Discipleship Journey: Consider how you were discipled or invited to follow Jesus. Was it through a personal decision or invitation? Reflect on past models of evangelism you've used or been taught. Journal your thoughts and feelings about this experience.

Create a Relationship Chart: Draw a network of your relationships on a large piece of paper. Visualize how people are connected to each other. Consider how the gospel could spread through these connections and groups of people.

CHAPTER FIFTEEN:ONGOING

Scripture: *When the apostles returned, they reported to Jesus what they had done. Then he took them with him and they withdrew by themselves to a town called Bethsaida.* – Luke 9:10

Key Concepts:
- Training disciples is a process, not a program or event.
- Develop life-on-life relationships that go deeper than a meeting or a one-hour call.
- Making disciples is an ongoing process of teaching, skill training, practice, modeling in the field, debriefing, training again, sending out again, and also of eating, playing, and worshipping together.

JOURNAL ABOUT THESE QUESTIONS:

HAVE YOU EVER FELT YOUR DISCIPLE-MAKING WAS FINISHED AFTER LEADING SOMEONE THROUGH A CLASS OR PROGRAM? HOW DOES THIS CHAPTER CHALLENGE THAT MINDSET?

IDENTIFY THREE TO FIVE INDIVIDUALS YOU'RE MENTORING TO BECOME DISCIPLE-MAKERS. HOW CAN YOU BETTER OBSERVE THEIR LIVES AND 'LISTEN FOR OPPORTUNITIES' AS YOU GUIDE THEM?

IF YOU DO NOT HAVE ANYONE YOU ARE TRAINING LIFE-ON-LIFE, WHAT STEP WILL YOU TAKE TO MOVE FORWARD IN THIS AREA?

SUGGESTED ACTION STEPS:

Reflect on Past Groups: Think about the last discipleship class or small group you led or attended. Did relationships extend beyond the meetings? If not, what changes could foster deeper connections? Next time, actively "listen" for opportunities.

Engage in Disciple-Making: Invite someone to join you for a disciple-making activity this week. Take a prayer walk in your area, start spiritual conversations at a mall, or seek out a new "Person of Peace" nearby through "treasure hunting".

LESSON FOUR

NOTES

ACTION STEPS

Which Action Steps did you work on this week? Be ready to share with your group about at least two of them and how they went for you.

This week, add In your own action steps you have committed to from your lessons.

ACTION STEP CHECKLIST

- [ ] Establish a new prayer habit.
- [ ] Use a prayer app.
- [ ] Attend a different prayer meeting.
- [ ] Reflect on your discipleship journey.
- [ ] Create a relationship chart.
- [ ] Reflect on past groups.
- [ ] Engage In disciple-making.
- [ ]
- [ ]
- [ ]

NOTES

Understand prayer as a vital ministry rather than just a preparatory activity. Explore various prayer methods like prayer walking and maintaining a Lost & Saved list to foster deep, transformative prayer for your community's spiritual needs.

LESSON FIVE

Watch Video 5- Resources & Methods: Needs & Easy Mindsets

DISCUSSION:

ASK YOURSELF

WRITE YOUR ANSWERS HERE...

Prayer Requests. What are some personal prayer needs you have this week? If In a group setting, how can you pray for your group this week?

Content Review.
What stood out to you in the chapters we read this week?

Action Item Review. Share about any application or action steps taken after reading. Discuss how these steps went, what went well, and what challenges were faced.

THIS WEEK'S ASSIGNMENTS:

1 **TO READ:**
Read chapters 16 and 17 (pages 156-175).

2 **TO JOURNAL:**
Journal about the questions at the end of the chapters.

3 **FOR GROUPS:**
Choose at least 2 suggested action steps in the workbook to report back to the group about.

CHAPTER SIXTEEN:NEEDS

Scripture: *In the midst of a very severe trial, their overflowing joy and their extreme poverty welled up in rich generosity.* −2 Corinthians 8:2

Key Concepts:
• Ownership above offers. Build ownership to solve problems rather than bringing in outside offers of help.
• Look for local resources in the harvest itself. This encourages dignity and sustainability of the future movement.
• The best way to destroy poverty is through teaching the poor to give generously.

JOURNAL ABOUT THESE QUESTIONS:

> **READ LUKE 9:3 AND LUKE 10:4. HOW DOES THIS INFORM YOUR THINKING ABOUT DISCIPLE-MAKING AND MISSIONS? IN WHAT WAYS CAN WE APPLY THIS IN MODERN TIMES?**

> **WHAT IS THE DIFFERENCE BETWEEN RELIEF AND DEVELOPMENT? WHAT DID YOU LEARN FROM WHAT JEAN JOHNSON SHARED WITH THE INDIAN GROUP OF CHURCH PLANTERS?**

> **WHY COULD IT BE DANGEROUS TO BRING MONEY FROM OUTSIDE THE MOVEMENT TO BUILD BUILDINGS OR PAY SALARIES?**

SUGGESTED ACTION STEPS:

Identify Local Assets: List the resources and strengths present in your community. How can these local assets be used to spread the gospel instead of relying on external resources? Discuss this with a friend or team member.

Facilitate a Giving Activity: Host a giving session in your disciple-making group, church, or with friends. Instead of monetary donations, invite everyone to bring an item to give away. Place these items in the center, pray over them, then each person takes one item to give to someone else in the group.

CHAPTER SEVENTEEN:EASY

Scripture: *The Advocate, the Holy Spirit, whom the Father will send in my name, will teach you all things and will remind you of everything I have said to you.* –John 14:26

Key Concepts:
• Keep discipleship easy and actionable.
• It isn't about how many truths you make people understand, it is about how far one truth will spread to others.
• Short, bite-sized, just-in-time, skill-based, and practical training is more effective for disciple multiplication.
• We must be willing to ruthlessly evaluate training methods in light of fruit and impact on disciple-making and the lost.

JOURNAL ABOUT THESE QUESTIONS:

Do you have a strong emotional attachment or loyalty to a particular training model? We often feel sentimental about our training methods because of the impact they had on our lives.

How open are you to a new way of thinking and working when it comes to equipping workers for the harvest?

Pause and ask God for guidance. Seek His light on areas where you may be overly loyal and need to change. What adjustments will you make in your disciple training?

SUGGESTED ACTION STEPS:

Revise Discipleship Training: *Reevaluate your discipleship programs based on the insights from this chapter. What changes can you implement to make them more field-based, practical, and timely? Pray about developing a simpler, more accessible training that new disciples can immediately use to train others in their faith journey.*

Learn from Children's Education: *Visit a kids' church program or elementary school classroom. Observe how teachers simplify and apply practical concepts for children. Consider adapting these methods for training adults.*

Pray and Surrender: *Reflect on your emotional attachment to specific discipleship training methods. Surrender this to God in prayer and express openness to new approaches that may foster faster disciple multiplication.*

NOTES

_____
_____
_____
_____
_____
_____
_____
_____
_____
_____
_____
_____
_____
_____
_____
_____
_____
_____
_____
_____
_____

ACTION STEPS

Which Action Steps did you work on this week? Be ready to share with your group about at least two of them and how they went for you.

This week, add In your own action steps you have committed to from your lessons.

ACTION STEP CHECKLIST

- ☐ Identify local assets.

- ☐ Facilitate a giving activity.

- ☐ Revise discipleship training.

- ☐ Learn from children's education.

- ☐ Pray and surrender.

- ☐
- ☐
- ☐
- ☐

NOTES

Emphasize local ownership and sustainability in your disciple-making efforts. Seek to empower individuals by utilizing local resources and encouraging self-reliance. Discuss how teaching generosity can lead to holistic community transformation.

LESSON SIX

Watch Video 6- Multiplication and Worship: Equippers & Relevant Mindsets

DISCUSSION:

ASK YOURSELF

WRITE YOUR ANSWERS HERE...

Prayer Requests. What are some personal prayer needs you have this week? If In a group setting, how can you pray for your group this week?

Content Review.
What stood out to you in the chapters we read this week?

Action Item Review. Share about any application or action steps taken after reading. Discuss how these steps went, what went well, and what challenges were faced.

THIS WEEK'S ASSIGNMENTS:

1 **TO READ:**
Read Chapters 18, 19 and the Conclusion (pages 175-192).

2 **TO JOURNAL:**
Journal about the questions at the end of the chapters.

3 **FOR GROUPS:**
Choose at least 2 suggested action steps in the workbook and be ready to share about them In your group.

4 **TO READ:**
Read through Appendix 2, 3, and 4 (pages 223-238)

5 **PRAYER:**
Pray about what God wants you to do individually and corporately with your group to move forward in disciple-making and multiplication in your own context. Be ready to discuss that.

CHAPTER EIGHTEEN:EQUIPPERS

Scripture: *Christ himself gave the apostles, the prophets, the evangelists, the pastors and teachers, to equip his people for works of service, so that the body of Christ may be built up.* —Ephesians 4:11-12

Key Concepts:
- Equip equippers. Disciple disciple-makers.
- Our most important task is to train others until they can do what we do.
- Ephesians 4:11–12 teaches us to equip the saints for the work of service, not to do all the work ourselves.

JOURNAL ABOUT THESE QUESTIONS:

HOW HAS THIS CHAPTER CHALLENGED YOUR UNDERSTANDING OF THE ROLE OF THOSE WITH MINISTERIAL GIFTS AND RESPONSIBILITIES? WHAT NEW INSIGHTS HAVE YOU GAINED?

WHO CAN YOU TAKE STEPS TO EQUIP AND TRAIN THIS WEEK? HOW CAN YOU BECOME A TRAINER OF TRAINERS?

WHAT QUESTIONS DOES FRED'S EXAMPLE BRING TO MIND? IN WHAT WAYS CAN YOU RELATE TO HIS STORY? WHAT COULD YOU APPLY TO YOUR SITUATION?

SUGGESTED ACTION STEPS:

Develop Your Gifting: *Think about your main spiritual gift. Who are you mentoring to develop the same gift? Identify someone you can encourage and train in this area. Reach out to them and invite them to share your ministry role or platform in some capacity.*

Delegate Responsibility: *Delegate at least one responsibility (with authority) to someone this month. Commit to supporting and guiding them in their new role. Empower others to empower more.*

CHAPTER NINETEEN:RELEVANT

Scripture: *Speak to one another with psalms, hymns and spiritual songs. Sing and make music in your hearts to the Lord.* −Ephesians 5:19, BSB

Key Concepts:
- Participatory, culturally relevant worship spreads far.
- Every disciple needs to grow as an active worshipper both personally and corporately.
- Indigenous worship touches and transforms the heart more deeply than translated or imported Western songs do.
- There are many different non-musical ways to encourage participatory worship in a group.

JOURNAL ABOUT THESE QUESTIONS:

ARE THERE WAYS THIS CHAPTER HAS EXPANDED YOUR UNDERSTANDING OF WORSHIP? WHAT WAS A NEW IDEA FOR YOU?

EVALUATE YOUR CHURCH OR SMALL GROUP'S CURRENT WORSHIP TIMES. HOW SIMPLE AND REPRODUCIBLE ARE THEY? WHAT COULD YOU EXPERIMENT WITH THAT WOULD BE MORE SO?

THINK OF A NEW AND CREATIVE WAY TO WORSHIP GOD, EITHER ALONE OR WITH OTHERS. SHARE IT WITH YOUR GROUP OR JOURNAL ABOUT IT.

SUGGESTED ACTION STEPS:

Explore New Worship: *Try worshipping in a different way than usual. For instance, write a poem, paint, compose a song, arrange flowers, carve a Bible verse in wood, or any other creative activity. Better yet, do it with a friend or two.*

Non-Musical Worship Experiment: *Explore a non-musical worship activity. Sit in a circle with your group and complete the phrase, "The thing I love most about Jesus is _____. How about you?" Let each person share their response before moving to the next.*

ACTION STEPS

Which Action Steps did you work on this week? Be ready to share with your group about at least two of them and how they went for you.

This week, add In your own action steps you have committed to from your lessons.

ACTION STEP CHECKLIST

- ☐ Develop your gifting.
- ☐ Delegate responsibility.
- ☐ Explore new worship.
- ☐ Non-musical worship experiment.
- ☐
- ☐
- ☐
- ☐
- ☐

NOTES

Focus on equipping others to multiply disciples. Reflect on Ephesians 4:11–12 and the importance of training disciple-makers who can, in turn, train others. Shift from doing all the work yourself to empowering others for service and leadership.

NOTES

CONCLUSION

As you conclude this journey through The Multipliers Mindset, we trust you've gained valuable insights into transforming discipleship. Now, take a moment to consider the new perspectives and practical steps you've embraced. Commit to applying these learnings in your daily life and ministry. Share these transformative ideas with others, fostering a community dedicated to effective disciple-making and multiplication. Together, let's continue to sow seeds of faith and watch God multiply His impact through each of us.

WHAT ARE THE MOST IMPORTANT NEW INSIGHTS YOU HAVE GAINED FROM THIS BOOK?

WHAT ACTION STEPS WILL YOU TAKE TO PUT WHAT YOU LEARNED INTO PRACTICE THIS COMING MONTH OR YEAR?

WHO WILL YOU SHARE THESE IDEAS AND ACTIONS WITH?

And Jesus came and said to them, 'All authority in heaven and on earth has been given to me. Go therefore and make disciples of all nations, baptizing them in the name of the Father and of the Son and of the Holy Spirit, teaching them to observe all that I have commanded you. And behold, I am with you always, to the end of the age.'. –Matthew 28:18-20 ESV

OTHER RESOURCES

Explore more resources to deepen your journey in disciple-making, including our podcast for ongoing inspiration and courses like 'Getting Started in Disciple Making Movements' for further learning and application. Scan the QR codes to access these valuable resources conveniently.

DARE TO MULTIPLY PODCAST

on Apple Podcast

on YouTube

on Spotify

Follow us @daretomultiply

OTHER RESOURCES

Explore more resources to deepen your journey in disciple-making, including our podcast for ongoing inspiration and courses like 'Getting Started in Disciple Making Movements' for further learning and application. Scan the QR code to access this valuable resource conveniently.

AN ONLINE COURSE

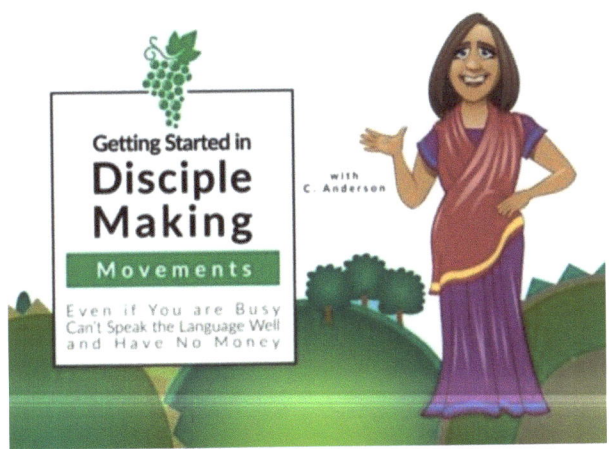

GETTING STARTED IN DISCIPLE MAKING MOVEMENTS ONLINE COURSE

Follow us @daretomultiply

OTHER RESOURCES

Explore more resources to deepen your journey in disciple-making, including our podcast for ongoing inspiration and courses like 'Getting Started in Disciple Making Movements' for further learning and application. Scan the QR codes to access these valuable resources conveniently.

BOOKS BY CYNTHIA & OTHERS WE RECOMMEND

VIEW OUR FULL RESOURCE LIST

Follow us @daretomultiply